The Conflict Resolution Library™

Dealing with Showoffs

• Elizabeth Vogel •

The Rosen Publishing Group's
PowerKids Press™
New York

For Java Bean, a born showoff

Published in 2000 by The Rosen Publishing Group, Inc.
29 East 21st Street, New York, NY 10010

Copyright © 2000 by The Rosen Publishing Group, Inc.

All rights reserved. No part of this book may be reproduced in any form without permission in writing from the publisher, except by a reviewer.

Photo Illustrations by Shalhevet Moshe

First Edition

Layout and design: Erin McKenna

Vogel, Elizabeth.
　Dealing with showoffs / by Elizabeth Vogel.
　　　　p.　cm. — (The conflict resolution library)
　Includes index.
　Summary: Discusses why people show off, what to do if a showoff makes you feel bad, and how to change if you are the showoff.
　　ISBN 0-8239-5412-9 (lib. bdg. : alk. paper)
　1. Attention-seeking—Juvenile literature.　[1. Attention-seeking.]　I. Title. II. Series.
BF637.A77V64　1999
302.5'4—dc21
98-35656
CIP

Manufactured in the United States of America

Contents

1	What Is a Showoff?	5
2	Why Do People Show Off?	6
3	How Do You Feel?	9
4	Roberta and Mrs. Klein	10
5	Self-esteem	13
6	Dustin and Holly	14
7	When Friends Show Off	17
8	Are You a Showoff?	18
9	Not a Showoff Anymore	21
10	Feeling Proud	22
	Glossary	23
	Index	24

What Is a Showoff?

Have you ever seen someone show off? A friend might have bragged to you about the new toy she got for her birthday, or maybe she kept telling you how her gymnastics teacher always says she is the best student in the class. A showoff is someone who brags or tries to show how good he is at something. Sometimes showoffs look for too much attention. They try to take attention away from others. Showoffs can make others feel bad by bragging so much, even if they don't mean to.

◀ *Showoffs are not very good at sharing attention. Bragging makes them feel important.*

Why Do People Show Off?

Sometimes it's hard to understand why someone shows off. Maybe your friend feels sorry for himself because his project didn't win a prize at the science fair. Maybe he is **embarrassed** that the judges didn't think his work was good enough. He may want to prove to you and to himself that he is special. He might brag about how his mom got him great new in-line skates. He wants to feel good about himself. The problem is that he talks so much about himself that he doesn't listen to you.

This boy brags about his new in-line skates. He makes his friend, who doesn't have a pair, feel bad. ▶

How Do You Feel?

Showoffs can make you feel bad about yourself. They tell you how great they are. You might feel angry when someone brags all the time. He may make you feel **ashamed** because you don't have cool clothes or because your parents don't have a fancy car. You might also feel **jealous**. Showoffs can make you feel like you're not good enough. Try to remember that you are. You, your family, and your friends all know that you are good at many things. It doesn't matter what a showoff thinks!

◄ *A showoff might make you feel unimportant because he makes you feel like you are not good at something.*

Roberta And Mrs. Klein

Roberta was showing off and making too much noise in Mrs. Klein's classroom. She didn't understand the math lesson, but she felt better when she made her classmates laugh. Her teacher asked her why she was **disrupting** the class. Roberta told her she was feeling **frustrated** with math. Mrs. Klein said that she understood, but that Roberta should raise her hand and ask a question in class instead of making jokes and showing off. Roberta agreed. Mrs. Klein said she would give Roberta the extra help that she needed.

After getting in trouble for showing off, Roberta told her teacher that she didn't mean to disturb the class.

Self-esteem

Many showoffs have low **self-esteem**. Self-esteem is how a person feels about herself. Sometimes showoffs brag to make themselves feel better. A showoff might need help from parents, teachers, and friends to learn how to increase her self-esteem. One way a person can feel better about herself is to think about all the things she does well. Another way is by working to accomplish something. She could try hard to do a good job in her reading group. The more a person **achieves**, the higher a person's self-esteem.

◀ *This girl practices her singing so she can try out for the school play.*

Dustin and Holly

Dustin was the last person picked for the basketball team during gym class. He was very embarrassed. On the court, Dustin kept telling everyone about his amazing baseball card collection. The other kids just wanted to play the game. They didn't realize how badly Dustin felt about being picked last. They just wanted him to stop showing off. His friend Holly told him to stop talking about his card collection and start playing basketball. Dustin realized that if he stopped bragging and played the game, he might get better.

After the game, Holly told Dustin that bragging wouldn't make him better at basketball. She offered to help him practice shooting baskets.

When Friends Show Off

Should you tell your friend if he is a showoff? You should if his **behavior** upsets you. Maybe a friend gets to visit his dad in another town every weekend. When he comes to school on Monday, he brags about all the fun things they did together. You could say, "I like hearing about your weekend, but I'd also like to share my good news from the weekend. When you don't listen to me, it feels like you are not interested in what I have to say." Tell him that you care about him, but that friendship takes caring from both people.

◀ *If you have a friend who shows off, it's a good idea to talk to him and tell him how this makes you feel.*

Are You a Showoff?

Could you be a showoff? If you always talk about the great things you have or can do, you might be one. Maybe you show off because you feel left out of things. Maybe you feel like no one is paying enough attention to you. Talk to an adult about how you feel. Your parents, teachers, or babysitter can help you find another way to feel better about yourself. Find a new club you'd like to join. Teach a friend how to do something that you can do. If you stop showing off, you can start having more fun with your friends.

This boy talks to his mom about what he can do to stop showing off and start feeling good about himself. ▶

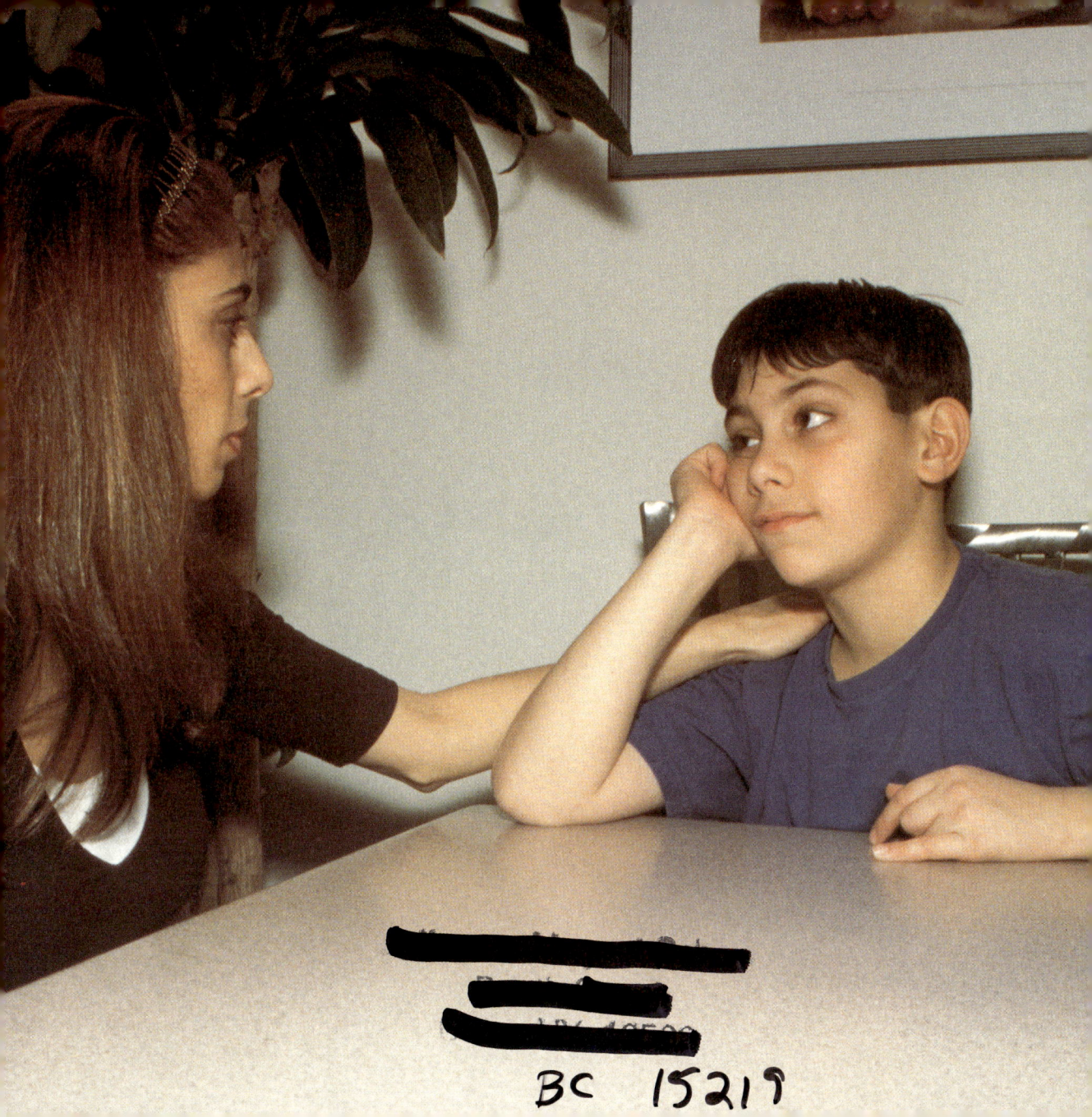

Not a Showoff Anymore

If you think you are a showoff, you can do things to change this. One way to stop being a showoff is to stop trying to get attention all the time. If your friend wants to tell you about his camping trip, then you should listen to him instead of talking about yourself. Sometimes you should get other people's attention and sometimes you should give your attention to them. It could be that you don't mean to show off, you just forget to listen to what other people have to say. Try to remember to ask other people about themselves.

◀ *Good friends share time together and listen to each other's feelings and thoughts.*

Feeling Proud

You can be proud of yourself without being a showoff. When you do well on your math test in school or win an award at camp, it's okay to tell people about it. There is a difference between showing off and being proud of yourself. Showoffs are just trying to get attention. Being proud means you want to share an **achievement** with someone who cares about you. When two friends can share all the good things that they do, their friendship grows stronger.

Glossary

achieves (uh-CHEEVZ) To do or accomplish by one's own efforts.
achievement (uh-CHEEV-ment) Something that is done with hard work and courage.
ashamed (uh-SHAYMD) Feeling uncomfortable or uneasy because you think you did something wrong.
behavior (bee-HAY-vyur) How a person acts.
disrupting (dis-RUHP-ting) Interrupting someone or something in a rude way.
embarrassed (em-BAYR-est) To feel uneasy or upset about something.
frustrated (FRUS-tray-ted) When you feel angry or sad because you cannot do anything about a certain situation.
jealous (JEH-lus) To feel upset because you want to be like someone else or have what someone else has.
self-esteem (SELF ih-STEEM) How someone feels about himself or herself.

Index

A
achieve, 13
achievements, 22
anger, 9
ashamed, 9
attention, 5, 18, 21, 22

B
behavior, 17
bragging 5, 6, 9, 13, 14, 17

D
disrupting, 10

E
embarrassed, 6, 14

F
feeling left out, 18
friendship, 17, 22
frustrated, 10

J
jealous, 9

L
listening, 6, 17, 21

P
proud, 22

S
self-esteem, 13
sharing, 22

T
talking, 6, 17, 18, 21
teaching, 18